Watching for the Kingfisher

Watching for the Kingfisher

Incorporating Candles and Kingfishers,
Flashes of Brightness, and some new poems

Ann Lewin

British Library Cataloguing in Publication data

A catalogue record for this book is available
from the British Library

ISBN 1 85852 256 0

First published by Inspire
4 John Wesley Road
Werrington
Peterborough PE4 6ZP

Printed and bound in Great Britain by
Stanley L. Hunt (Printers) Ltd, Rushden, Northants

Foreword

I'd written my sermon for Archbishop Robert Runcie's funeral but I didn't know how to finish it. (Endings can be just as problematic for sermons as they are for novels or poems.) It needed something elegant and generous to express what I believed was so special about this man of God who delighted in life and in people.

I found myself browsing through Ann Lewin's poetry for inspiration. And there it was. After Word. It said what needed to be said, and with an appropriateness that was uncanny. We even buried Robert Runcie 'on the seventh day'. We laid him to rest, as the poem says, 'well content'. I quoted the poem in full. Ann heard about it and we've been in touch ever since.

It was no accident that I turned to Ann's poetry. Another bishop had introduced me to her writing a couple of years before. He did me a very good turn. Ann's poems trigger my thinking and my prayers. I admire her craft as a wordsmith. She's helped me sharpen any skills I may have in that area. When I read her poetry I find, to use Ian Ramsey's phrase, 'the penny drops'. She writes of her life experience and brings a fresh perspective to gospel stories and biblical characters, yet one that somehow seems strangely familiar. I feel as if I'm reading what I've always known though never quite been able to articulate. She helps illuminate reality with new shafts of light.

Ann's poetry always leaves me feeling I inhabit a larger world as a result of reading it. One of my children, when just three years old, asked me, 'Does God grow?' At the time I didn't think he wanted a

detailed examination of one of the issues at the heart
of process theology. But I've never forgotten the
question. I was reminded of it time and time again
when I read this new volume of Ann's poetry. I know
that, through her, my delight in the unexpected
graces of our daring God has grown. I've learned too
that poems don't have to be long to be profound.

I hope this new collection will introduce Ann's poetry
to many other people. I'm sure it will win her new
admirers. Even better, it will enlarge sympathies and
help our vision of God to grow.

+ Graham Norvic:

The Rt Revd Graham James
Bishop of Norwich

Preface

The title of this book describes two related activities: birdwatching, and prayer.

I began to make the connection through the experience of *not* seeing a kingfisher. Everyone else staying in the house where I was a guest saw it, but I, the self-confessed birdwatcher, didn't. It was frustrating, to say the least! But one morning, when I was haunting the lake unsuccessfully yet again, I realised that I was being told something important about prayer, and the poem 'Disclosure' from which the title comes, was the result.

Prayer, the expression of our desire for God and our relationship with God, is not something we control, it is what we are drawn to. It is the practice of being there, ready to receive God's gift of himself, not being put off if nothing much seems to be going on, or if conditions seem to be distinctly unfavourable, but waiting, alert and expectant.

Birdwatchers are in a sense contemplatives. They spend quite a lot of time waiting. They learn about times and seasons and habitats; they provide themselves with warm clothing and wet-weather gear so that they don't just give up when the weather is challenging; they acquire equipment to help them focus and identify what they are looking at. Sometimes watchers are rewarded with the sight of a rare bird, mostly they have to be content with more common species, but always they learn something. One of the first things they learn is that birds have their own lives, and don't appear just because we want them to: sometimes when watchers go out they see practically nothing, and sometimes they see birds they don't expect.

Birds are always around – we have to get into the habit of keeping our eyes open so that we notice them. We have to be ready to meet God in unlikely places too, as well as obvious ones. His coming, like the arrival of a kingfisher, is always gift. And because God's habitat is the whole of creation, (not just the church!), our experience and circumstances as well as the more focused times of prayer, Bible reading and worship, are where God comes to us.

The contents of this book describe some of my moments of encounter and insight – kingfisher moments, flashes of brightness which give encouragement. I hope they will resonate with yours, and perhaps give you some kingfisher moments too.

Ann Lewin
Southampton 2004

Contents

Entrance

Pause at the threshold
Of the sacred space;
Bow low.
Prepare for fresh
Encounter
With the Holy One.

Stage fright

It's often somewhat
Disconcerting when
God takes us at our word.
'Take me and use me,'
We say, meaning it;
But when God does,
There is a moment of surprise,
Perhaps terror, 'Me?'

Then, our 'Yes' loved from us,
Comes the realisation
That the opportunity is gift,
The outcome held in grace.

Truth

For some, Truth is a fortress, square and strong,
In which, once entered, safety lies.
Only like-minded people dwell there, none disturb
The calm and certain sureties of belief.
Outside, the world pursues its way, its noise and
Clamour offering small attraction to those
Whose knowledge keeps them safe beyond the
Drawbridge of conviction. If any try to breach the
Bastions of tradition, they are repelled with
Boiling scorn. Truth is impregnable.

For others, Truth is both journey and
Discovery, a Way which leads and
Urges without rest.
No castle for retreat, but
Camps, where fellow pilgrims join
To take refreshment in each other's
Company. Assorted in experience, they
Enrich, enlighten, challenge and
Go on to further exploration.
Travelling light. Knowing that in this life
All is provisional; seeking fulfilment,
The end and explanation of the quest.

Moving mountains

Only have faith ...
But that's the problem;
How much do we need?
What if we haven't enough?

The questions miss the point:
Faith is not a commodity
To be possessed,
A bargaining counter
Used to get things done;
Faith is the orientation
Of our lives, a gift
Which shifts perceptions,
Takes us deeper
Into the mystery of God.

Kaleidoscope

Held in a circle,
Trinity mirrors reflect
Changing perceptions
Of relationships
In ever-changing sequence.
Fragile connections
Need to be broken
To re-form in different shapes,
Offering new insights.

Myriad fragments –
Meaningless life-puzzle or
On-the-way patterns?

Odyssey

I have not always been dancing in sunlight.
There has been shadow too, death and
Resurrection, rehearsals for the
Final curtain.
Death painful, mocking scornfully at
Life's endeavour. Resurrection
Dawning realisation of endless
Possibilities.

Psalm 84

Use this?
You must be joking.
Who could find comfort
In such bitter water?
Rather, let this cup
Pass from me,
This cannot be your will.
Why should life be
Like this?
Why me?

Why not?

And anyway,
There's not much choice.
It's this or nothing.
Use it for a well,
And see what happens.

In the heat of struggle
It is not sweetness which refreshes,
But the astringent bitterness
Which sets the teeth on edge.
Drink deep, and find
Mysterious refreshment.

Psalm 84.5-6

The next four poems were written in response to the experience of having breast cancer.

Unwelcome visitor

A needle in my breast,
A word, *malignant,*
And a sword pierced my soul.

Crabbed insidiousness,
Who gave you leave
To enter and attempt
Possession?
Don't get too comfortable,
You are not welcome.
Eviction follows swiftly
On this notice.

Marked for life

Ash Wednesday, cross-shaped mark
Remember you are dust ...
A touch that brands and heals,
The mark, like Cain's, a sign of
God's protection.

And now, another
Reminder of mortality:
Lines drawn for radiotherapy.
Could these too be
A sign of God's protection,
Focusing healing rays
Not coming gently
But with searing power?

Come, Holy Spirit,
Come in these rays
To cleanse and heal.

Dark moments

'All shall be well' ...
She* must have said that
Sometimes through gritted teeth.
Surely she knew the moments
When fear gnaws at trust,
The future loses shape,
Gethsemane?

The courage that says
'All shall be well'
Doesn't mean feeling no fear,
But facing it, trusting
God won't let go.

'All shall be well'
Doesn't deny present experience,
But roots it deep
In the faithfulness of God,
Whose will and gift is life.

Julian of Norwich

Vulnerable

We've been here before, Lord,
You and I. A situation
Not of your will, and
Certainly not my choice.
I can't believe that you send
Suffering, and I don't want it.
We look at each other,
And feel the pain
That this is how it is.

I do not acquiesce
Without complaint;
And yet the words die on my lips,
For in response you come
With wounded hands
And cradle me in love.

Healing

What if pain does not go,
What then? Scars can be
Touched to raw response in
Unexpected moments
Long after the event which
Caused them, nerve ends twitch
Perhaps for ever after
Amputation.

Healing is not achieved
Without some cost. It
May not mean the end of
Pain. Healing can hurt
Just like fresh wounds,
As pockets of poison are
Lanced, or lesions cut to
Allow more flexibility. For
Healing is not going back
To what one was before,
It is a growing on
To a new stage of being,
Through many deaths and
Resurrections being set free.

Astringent sweetness

I watched the bees
Working the teasel heads,
And marvelled
That from such
Sharp encounter
They could draw
Sweetness.

Could it be so for us,
That holding on through
Pain, our difficulties
Will in time yield
Nourishment?

The prayer we offer

Not for ease? Why not?
What's wrong with ease?
For most of us the
Problem is not self-indulgence,
But that we allow ourselves too little.
Prohibitions, counsels of perfection,
Drive us and load us up with guilt.

Time enough for courageous living
And all that rock-smiting.
Let's rest and wander in green pastures
When we find them, make the space
To let ourselves be loved;
Build up our strength
And grow in confidence;
Drink living water springing in
Great fountains;
Feed on the Bread of Life which
Satisfies.

Then we shall have provision
For the journey, and at last
Arrive, not too unpractised
In the art of resting
In his presence.

A response to the hymn
'Father, hear the prayer we offer'

Telephone

Shrill disembodied clamour for attention,
Paying scant heed to previous engagement,
Why should I answer you?

If what you bring is urgent,
It will come again more opportunely,
Otherwise, I will not grieve.

Remember, you are servant,
Not my master.
You ring at my command,
I will not run at yours.

Meditation

Cows get it about right.
Unhurried pace and gentle curiosity,
The natural rhythms of their day,
Giving them ample time to chew things over.
We could do worse than stand around like cows.

Answer

I will answer the 'phone this day
In the power of the sacred Three.

The love of God
    be 'twixt me and each caller;
The welcome of Christ
    in me and my listening;
The Spirit's wisdom
    in me and my words;
The blessing of God
    on each one who hears me.

I will answer the 'phone this day
In the name of the sacred Three.

Quaker Meeting

Silence flowed round, enfolding us.
Sounds became distant,
A buzzing fly, a telephone,
Irrelevant.

Stillness.

A petal dropped onto
The polished surface,
Reflected in silence.

No movement.

Centreing down through
Our own preoccupations,
A handful of people,
Disparate, fragmented,
Finding a common unity
Where the Spirit moves
Below all speech.

Waiting.

Another petal fell into the
Silence, restful but disturbing.
Not the uneasy silence of
A breakdown in transmission,
But slow, prayerful
Deliberate pondering.

Half an hour longer, then,
A word.

On the surface,
Nothing much happened:
A fly buzzed in the window,
A telephone rang,
A petal fell onto
The polished surface.
But deep down, a change,
New understanding,
Resolution.

And peace went with us
When we left that place.

Written after Meeting at the Blue Idol Meeting House, Thakeham, where William Penn used to worship.

Be still

You do not have to look for anything,
Just look.
You do not have to listen for
Specific sounds,
Just listen.
You do not have to accomplish anything,
Just be.

And in the looking
And the listening
And the being,
Find
Me.

Retreat

Time out of time,
Resting ...
Drifting on Spirit's breath.

Cana revisited

Can you make wine of this?
Routine of work, or lack of it;
Relationships or brokenheartedness;
Struggle to tease out meaning in the dark;
Can these be changed?
If ordinary existence
Is poured out to be used,
Could you perform
Another miracle?

Perhaps the wonder is, being faithless,
We turn the wine of our potential to
Plain water.

John 2.1-11

Job share

The yoke is easy, but it's still
A yoke, smooth-shaped for work.
We chafe and struggle,
Longing to be free, yet
Double-yoked with
Christ who takes the strain,
The burden is not less, but light,
Weight redistributed for ease.

Matthew 11.28-30

Trees

Bare tracery against a
Flawless sky; promise of
Spring, sap-rising, bursting
Into leaf; fullness of
Flower at summer's height;
Flowers, fruit and then
Fulfilment in the autumn
Fire. Symbol of life and
Death and resurrection,
Endlessly repeated,
Growing to completion.
Standing deep-rooted,
Moving with the wind,
Offering shelter and
Strength to all who come,
Embodying ageless wisdom.

Here I will rest, and let the
Silence penetrate my depths,
Giving me timeless space
To grow and be.

Cross tree

A tree is something
You have to
Get to the
Top of.
Jesus climbed his,
With some
Assistance,
And stayed there,
Fixed by love,
To set us free
From the
Mad rush
To dominate
Our fellows.

'Take up your
Cross,'
He said, 'and
Follow Me.'

Christ the tree

Deep-rooted in the
Love of God the Father,
Moving, responding to
The Spirit's power;
Drawing all people
By your ageless
Wisdom, giving
To all who come
Healing and strength;
Life bursting forth,
Disturbing, powerful;
Cut down,
But bearing fruit.

Here I will rest,
And wait until sap rises,
Your life in mine,
My resurrection.

Two trees

God did not say,
'You must not eat
Fruit of the Tree of Life.'
But burdened by guilt
At tasting the forbidden fruit
Of the other tree, our energy
Is spent in dealing with our
Dreadful knowledge of
Good and evil.

And all the while,
The Tree of Life offers us
Nourishment.

Eat its fruit, and live.

Genesis 2.9

20

Prayer tree

Prayer gives us rootedness,
Reaching out ...
Discovering in darkness
Sources of nourishment;
Pushing with patient insistence
Against obstacles;
Drawing from strange places
Strength for life that
Grows in light;
Holding us as we bend,
And when we break, offering
Hope, that from the
Unimaginable dark,
New shoots will spring.

Peace trees

To be in the presence of trees
Is to know peace.
The silent rhythm of their life,
Bringing maturity in due time,
Without anxiety or haste,
Calms our impatience;
Their solid strength, derived from
Hidden roots spreading much further
Than we ever know, gives us security;
Grace, beauty, shapeliness and form,
Delight our senses, soothe our
Fragile nerves, and bring refreshment.

Let us in turn be trees,
Growing in God's time to maturity,
Spreading our roots deep into springs of life,
Opening branches wide to all who come
Offering strength and healing through our
Peace.

Spring

Underneath winter's struggle for survival
Life waits to be born.
After long periods of apparent desolation
Shoots appear, and colour warms the earth,
Gladdening the heart with hope.
Buried beneath our fears, preoccupations,
Apparent deadness, Life waits:
The growing is in the waiting.

Elixir

It's not bad weather, only rain.
Philosophers once thought
Drops cupped in Lady's Mantle
Would become pure gold.
So our imagination can transform
Grey to a shade of silver, and see
Rainbow colours caught up in the sun.

Pilgrims

And now it seems, from every
Country's end, at spring of year
To Canterbury they wend.
No longer holy martyr for to seek,
But pilgrims still,
Searching for roots in ancient history;
Finding a curious peace as prayer
Rolls through the cathedral
Joining the stream of endless praise.
Then on their way, that bit being done,
Echoes of something greater whispering
In their minds, pulling them back
Disturbingly to – what was it
We felt then, touching us
Under the surface of the package tour?

Arrivals

A glimpse of a familiar shape
Out of the corner of my eye, and
Suddenly my heart leaps in
Delighted recognition – they've
Arrived. After the months of
Watching the pavement lest I slip,
Hunching myself against the cold,
It's time to open up to gentle warmth,
And scan the skies for confirmation.
There they are, in growing numbers
Curving and swirling through the air.
One swallow may not make a summer,
But he definitely makes it Spring.

Consider the birds

That's one command
I have no problem with.

I held a swallow once,
Knocked senseless by some accident;
Fragile body, tiny beating heart
Cupped in my hand. Then, restored,
With flirt of feathers,
Off to freedom flight.
I who have scarcely
Stirred beyond these shores,
Held one who, twice at least,
Had flown four thousand miles.
No map, no compass,
Only unerring inner certainty
Carrying him over land and ocean.
A moment to treasure.

Then there are sparrows,
So common we don't notice them;
Eight a penny, or perhaps ten
Since decimalisation.
I wonder why you didn't tell Job
To look at sparrows, instead of
Parading the juggernauts of your
Creation. After all,
Anyone could make a hippopotamus –
No finesse there, a lump with
Four legs and a great big head –
A child's production.
But a sparrow, there's craftsmanship:
Those shades of brown and gold,
Arranged and sculpted into
Subtly beautiful plumage,
Each one different;
The stocky bodies full of energy,
Brisk, going about their business,
Fighting, squabbling,
Caring for their young, chirping
In incessant cheerfulness.

In contrast to the heron,
Standing more still than a
Contemplative, alert,
Waiting for the moment.

And no-one could watch ducks,
Or, better still, listen to them,
Without believing in your sense of humour.

Kingfisher's glory, blackbird's song,
The marvel of flight itself ...
The list is endless.

And we more precious.
A mystery to ponder.

Matthew 6.26
Job 40.15-18

Daybreak

As at the dawn of creation,
The lake awaits light's coming;
Herons stand, grey wraiths
In the swirling mist;
Wing-stretchings, stirrings in
Undergrowth, greet the day;
Questioning chirps from a
Secret world swell to
Full throat's song
In the strengthening sun;
A kingfisher – glimpse of glory
Glancing in sunlight.
No wonder God rejoices:
It is very good.

Benedicite

Swans came this morning,
Curving whiteness
Reflected on the lake.
They stayed, feeding,
Delighting those who saw.
Then, with that slow,
Distinctive wing beat,
They flew,
Leaving a sadness
On the empty lake.
So beautiful,
They stir strange longings.
Will they return?
We would be honoured
To be chosen for such
Privilege.

Going to Lauds

The rooks swirled in the dawn sky,
Greeting each other and the day
In noisy Benedicite.
Like thoughts in disarray,
They flew, and perched,
And flew again,
Finding, apparently, any excuse ...
Then, just when it seemed
That all was stilled,
More birds arrived, and
Off they went in great
Cacophony, to fly and perch,
And fly again.
Eventually,
Negotiations finished,
We settled,
Precariously:
They to rookery, I to prayer.

Definition?

The dictionary definition of the word 'halcyon' refers to an ancient legend that the bird of that name, usually identified with a species of kingfisher, was able to charm the wind and waves at the time of the winter solstice, so that the sea was calm enough for her nest to float on the water; hence the use of the word to mean 'calm', as in 'halcyon days' – originally the 14 days around that solstice.

(Most kingfishers actually nest in holes in river banks.)

If the author of the story of Job had written about the kingfisher (see Job 38), he might have said something like this ...

Were you there when I stilled
the turbulent waters,
so that the halcyon could brood her young?
Were you there when her glory first shone forth;
can you count her jewelled feathers?
Can you capture her beauty,
or trace her darting flight?
Does your purpose guide her
when she parts the water,
spearing food for her clamorous young?

Who are you, then, to question your Creator,
Who holds the Kingfisher in his hand?

Disclosure

Prayer is like watching for the
Kingfisher. All you can do is
Be where he is likely to appear, and
Wait.
Often, nothing much happens;
There is space, silence and
Expectancy.
No visible sign, only the
Knowledge that he's been there,
And may come again.
Seeing or not seeing cease to matter,
You have been prepared.
But sometimes, when you've almost
Stopped expecting it,
A flash of brightness
Gives encouragement.

Angels

Flames of fire, shafts of illumination;
Disconcerting messengers of God;
Assuring a woman that she can give birth,
Telling a man that what she bears is
Gift from God; challenging us to
Look, and not seek life where only death
Is found; opening doors, surrounding us with
Care, surprising us into fresh understanding.

Annunciation

It was not the first time
You had been there waiting, wondering.
This time there was quickening of senses,
Certainty that you would give birth.
A flash of insight filling you with terror,
How could this be?

The disconcerting messenger insisted
What you would bear was gift of God.
No need to wonder how:
The grace you needed was already in you,
Slowly maturing to the point of birth.

No one told you then how birth is painful,
Creation tearing you to the core.
That would come later. For the present,
All that's needed is your *'Yes.'*

Written as a response to a Fra Angelico painting.

Mary

Full of grace …
I wonder what that felt like.
Was your acceptance swift
And total, meek as your
Stained glass image?
Or was it wrung from you
In sweat and agony of mind?
The God I know does not get
Submissions very easily,
But then I'm not a Saint.
Perhaps you weren't either,
Just an ordinary person,
Struggling to understand.
Has the adulation over the years
Been a bit of an embarrassment,
Imprisoning you in dogma,
Preventing us from seeing you
As you are?

The family, were they convinced?
And the neighbours? I've often
Wondered about that visit to
Elisabeth – was that to get you
Away from all the gossip, until
The wedding could be arranged
Discreetly? And what about Joseph?
He must have thought it
A fine kind of angel who'd visited you.

We'll never know – but whatever
Happened, I'm pretty sure
The sword that pierced your soul
Didn't wait for the crucifixion.
And I've got a feeling that
You watch with some sympathy
As we struggle with our
Mysteries and pain.

Get real

You always appear
Too good to be true, Mary.
We've pictured you always serene,
Never exasperated by a fractious child,
Apparently having no feelings.

But surely that initial *Yes* came
From a moment of overwhelming terror?
And the birth tore you to the core?
Didn't he ever cry, that baby,
Give you sleepless nights?
Didn't he irritate you,
That precocious son
Dismissing your anxiety with
Didn't you know? And later
That wounding question,
Who is my mother?
My mother would have told him ...
Perhaps you did too,
But it wasn't recorded.

Even at the end, you're pictured
Beautiful in your sorrow,
Holding your dead child.
Not like those ravaged faces
We see on our screens
Raging at the senseless
Killing of the innocent.

What's the reality?
Is it more like the aged Madonna,
Gaunt, face lined by experience;
With hint of an arthritic hip
Walking towards the complexities of life,
Away from cloistered peace?
Her hand is polished smooth
By the touch of countless hands.

'The Walking Madonna' *by Elizabeth Frink strides through the Close in Salisbury.*

Wachet auf

Advent.
Season when
Dual citizenship
Holds us in
Awkward tension.

The world, intent on
Spending Christmas,
Eats and drinks its way to
Oblivion after dinner.
The Kingdom sounds
Insistent warnings:
Repent, be ready,
Keep awake,
He comes.

Like some great fugue
The themes entwine:
The Christmas carols,
Demanding our attention
In shops and pubs,
Bore their insistent way
Through noise of traffic;
Underneath, almost unheard,
The steady solemn theme of
Advent.

With growing complexity,
Clashing, blending,
Rivals for our attention,
Themes mingle and separate,
Pulling us with increasing
Urgency,
Until in final resolution,
The end attained,
Harmony rests in aweful
Stillness, and
The child is born.

He comes,
Both Child and Judge.

And will he find us
Watching?

Advent Sunday 1986, after hearing the 'Chorale Prelude' *by Bach.*

Christmas rush

Ready for Christmas?
You're joking! With all
I've got to do,
I'll be lucky if
I'm ready by
This time next year.

Stir-up Sunday
Found me without even
The ingredients,
Let alone the time to
Stir them ...

The cards –
I was going to write
More than
'Hope all is well'
This year.
But I haven't ...

Shopping's a nightmare,
With all those people
Intent on spending
Christmas ...

Working out who's
Visiting who, and
Who'll be offended
If we don't ...

The tree, the decorations,
Enough food for the cat,
Not to mention us,
I'll never be ready.

But I'm certainly ready for
Christmas – that moment when
The world seems hushed
In silent expectation,
The light in the stable
Draws us from chaos
To the stillness of
God at the centre,
And love is born.

I'm longing for that.

Stir-up Sunday got its name from the opening words of the Prayer Book Collect for the last Sunday before Advent: 'Stir up, we beseech thee, O Lord, the wills of thy faithful people ...'

Traditionally it was used as a reminder that it was time to make the Christmas puddings.

Eye opener

Thought-stirring misprint:
Christ found 'in a manager'.
Real Incarnation!

Incarnation

He's grown, that Baby.
Not that most people have noticed.
He still looks the same,
Lying there in the straw, with
Animals and shepherds looking on.
He's safe there, locked in that moment
Where time met Eternity.

Reality of course is different,
He grew up, astonished people with his
Insight, disturbed them with
Ideas that stretched them into
New maturity.

Some found him
Much too difficult to cope with,
Nailed him down to fit their
Narrow minds.

We are more subtle,
Keep him helpless,
Refuse to let him be the Man he is,
Adore him as the Christmas Baby,
Eternally unable to grow up
Until we set him free.

By all means let us pause there
At the stable, and
Marvel at the miracle of birth.
But we'll never get to know
God with us, until we learn
To find him at the Inn,
A fellow guest who shares the joy and sorrow,
The Host who is the life we celebrate.

He's grown, that Baby.

Christmas Word

When he was born,
He couldn't speak a word,
That Word made flesh.
All he could do was cry
The human cry of hunger
And the need for love.
He had to learn his words
At Mary's knee and Joseph's bench;
Words of the Kingdom values
That informed their lives.
And when he spoke,
It was again Mary's Magnificat,
Turning our expectations upside down:
Good News of transformation.
God's Word, and ours
If we too give it flesh
And live Magnificat:
Meeting the human cry
Of hunger and the need for love.

Inn signs

There were two innkeepers.
Do you blame him, that first one,
For only offering an outhouse?
It was a busy time –
You know the pressures –
Important visitors arriving –
What else could he do?
He did at least make room.

The other, hardly noticed,
Might have opened his door
To real trouble, letting that
Good Samaritan drag him in.
Who else lurked in the shadows?
Quite a risk, getting involved.

Both offered space –
And life began to grow.
Were both inns called
The Birth of Hope?

Luke 2.7; 10.35

Nativity scene

'Crib figures, take care',
The notice said.

The power of your simplicity,
Grouped there in silent
Adoration, could leave us
Most dissatisfied. Take care –
We cannot bear too much
Uneasiness. But keep us
Mindful of the hope
Embodied in that child,
Lest we allow it to shatter
Like a Christmas toy. Above all,
Keep us from underestimating God,
Who, more than anything, took risks.

Christmas card

The figures are the same:
The tender curves of
A mother cradling her child.
But there is no breastful of milk
To satisfy this infant
Whose cries of hunger echo her own.
Their eyes look blankly
At a world which offers little hope.

Come on, ye faithful,
And all people of goodwill,
It is time to be midwives
For the love of God
Struggling again to birth;
Deliver healing
To our crying world.

Merry Christmas

At the heart of Christmas there was
Pain, bleeding and crying;
Love was with difficulty brought to birth.
Not to a sanitised stable did God come,
But to a world that needed mucking out;
His birth no tidy affair, but through
A single parent, in bed and breakfast
Shelter; an inconvenience, not welcomed
By bureaucrats with important business;
Acknowledged mainly by low-paid workers,
Foreign visitors, and animals.
The sequel: attempted murder, exile.

People wounded by indifference
Struggle to give love birth in the
Cold comfort of charity, largely
Unrecognised by those with power.
At the heart of Christmas, still there's
Pain, bleeding and crying,
A sword piercing the heart of God,
Opening the wounds of love.

Could we be midwives for the love of God,
Cradling that strength born in fragility,
Delivering healing to the crying world?

Why them?

God, you must weep to see
The massacre of different
Innocents.
Stick limbs on swollen bellies,
Faces old before their time,
Skin stretched on grinning skulls.

We sit before the screen
And watch them die;
And from the world,
Mingling with your tears,
Comes Rachel's anguished cry
Because they are not.

And we could have helped.

Holy Innocents: 28 December. Matthew 2.13-18.

Twelfth Night

It looks much as it did before,
Now that the cards and decorations
Have come down.
The furniture of life is back in place,
The old routine takes over.
But are we the same?
Is there no echo of the angels' song
Lifting our spirits, no stillness
In our hearts, reminding us that
We were there, just for a moment,
At that birth,
Catching a glimpse of glory?
Let's not put that away,
Tangled with tinsel, for another time.
Let's ponder in our hearts, like Mary,
And let the Child grow with us
Through the year.

Suitable presents

If it's the thought that counts,
What were they thinking of
To give him these, Gold
Frankincense and Myrrh?
Extraordinary gifts to give a child.

When Mary pondered, later, on these things,
I wonder if she thought that
These are given to all –
Gold: our potential, gifts that make us
Royal, each in our own domain;
Incense: our aspirations, prayers
And dreams, calling us on;
Myrrh: soothing healing for our pain.
Not gifts for children,
But, like him, we'll grow.

Senior moment

His parents brought him
In obedience to the Law,
A baby six weeks old,
To offer thanks and
Dedicate their son.
Nothing unusual –
But for Simeon and Anna,
Revelation.

Only mentioned once,
These two had been around
Waiting and watching
Prayerfully for years,
Longing to see salvation.
And patience was rewarded
When they saw the Child.
A moment of recognition,
And they spoke about
Fulfilment, theirs and his.
For once old people
Had the best lines.

Age does not have to mean
Diminishment. There may well be
Constraints, but there is also
Space and time for patient
Prayerful growth to
Wisdom's fruitfulness.

Luke 2.22-38

Candlemas Prayer

I left my candle burning. Lit from light
Borrowed from another, it stood there
Witness to Christ, Light of the world;
Prayer that light would overcome darkness.
As I left, another lit a candle from my light,
Dispelling gloom with added strength.
Who knows how many joined their light to those,
Or drew fresh courage from their company;
Who knows how many took a step, drawn by the
Light of Christ from darkness to new life?

Lord Christ, set me on fire.
Burn from me all that dims your light,
Kindle an answering flame in lives around;
That darkness may be driven back,
And glory stream into this world,
Transforming it with love.

Baptism

Birth by drowning,
Upheaval of a settled way of life.

All birth is dying,
A painful separation from the past.
Our first birth called us from
Security, to face the lifelong
Struggle to survive.
Our second, no less vigorously
Calls us to set out on our
Pilgrimage with Christ,
Finding in him, with all our
Fellow pilgrims, new insights
Into love, and truth and life.
A pilgrimage that daunts us
And excites us,
And will not let us rest till
We arrive. Our only certainty
God's promise, 'My love will hold you,
Do not be afraid.'

Ordinary Time

A vellum fragment of the Rule,
Cover and outer pages long since gone;
Nothing ornate, a working document,
Stained with use as well as time.

I held it, and I thought
Of all whose hands had held it too,
People like us, who through the years
Followed the daily discipline
Of prayer, a diverse company
Seeking God's mercy.

Wells Cathedral Library is home to a fragment of the Benedictine Rule, dated around 1000AD, probably originating at Glastonbury.

Simple Vows

Simple, not easy.
The economy of words
Belies the depth of the surrender;
No complicated debate about
How much to give:
Life stripped to the riches of poverty,
(Sustain me according to your promise)
The requirement is, everything.

The nails of obedience
Fastening me to this place
Scar like crucifixion
(That I may live).

Totally costly;
Totally rewarding;
(Let me not be disappointed
In my hope);

Simply all.

At Burford Priory, when two of the brothers renewed their Simple Vows, after promising obedience, stability and conversion of life, the rubric required them to stand with arms extended and say a verse from Psalm 119: 'Sustain me according to your promise that I may live; let me not be disappointed in my hope.'

Solemn Profession

The engagement is fulfilled
    that time of fearful, hopeful
    search, discovery
    has brought me to this place.

What I seek is here:
    the mercy of God enfolds me,
    draws me on to ever
    deeper trust.

With this ring –
    encircling of God's love,
    source of stability;
    unbroken bond
    within community;
    symbol of my desire
    to give myself –
what once was simple
now becomes a total offering:
    being refined like gold,
    eternally given and
    received and blessed.

Sustain me, O Lord,
according to your promise
that I may live:
let me not be disappointed
in my hope.

Written for three brothers who made their Profession in Solemn Vows, 28 May 1994.

In tune

Done your practice? Said your prayers?
Echoes from childhood, as though
Practice must be perfect, prayer complete.
Experience tells us neither satisfies
Till techniques spring to life.

Prayer is musicianship, a
Growing alertness to God's beat,
Drawn to the rhythm of his will,
Watching his cues for
Rest or entry; listening,
Aware of others' harmony, or
Seeking in discord sounds of
Resolution; accepting occasional
Transposition to enable others
To join in; through many modulations
Learning the beauty of the minor key
Offsetting major's splendour.
Then, secure, daring to improvise
Above the steady groundbass of God's love.

Prayer

A time of disengagement
From routine.
Desert. Emptiness.
Wordless waiting before
The mystery.
Nothing much happened:
No flash of insight,
No resolution of perplexity,
But deep down,
Shifting perceptions,
Something understood.

I beg your pardon

Easy for you to say, 'Forgive.'
But how can I forget that hurt,
Welcome that person?
Etched deeply in my memory,
I can't 'forget' as though
It never happened.

Can I then learn to remember?

There is a way that keeps the hurt alive,
Quick to imagine other grievances.
There is a way that's based on a pretence –
That all was for the best – failing to
Realise the gravity of the event, or
Take it seriously. 'It doesn't matter',
Said dismissively, diminishes the person
Asking pardon, as well as failing
To acknowledge hurt.
There is a way that says, 'Yes,
That was bad, it hurt, but now,
In fuller knowledge of each other,
Let's go ahead and set each other free
To build up trust and grow again in love;
Perhaps together, but perhaps apart,
Only without the rancour that destroys.'

For my salvation?

A shaft of light caught the crucifix in the chapel in Burford Priory, and started a train of thought ...

His bloodied knees
Caught my attention ...
I've grown accustomed
To the sight of blood
Pouring from thorn-crowned head
And marks of nails and spear:
The crucified Christ
Bearing the sins of the world.
A distant Christ, carrying
The big sins – murder,
Premeditated cruelty –
Other people's sins, not often mine.
(Although I have it in me.)

But the sore knees
Brought him close.
That blood comes from
Everyone's experience;
Tripped up by inattention,
Undue haste, or thoughtlessness,
We feel the sting.
Those sins I know,
Catching me unaware.

It was the weight of such sins
Caused him to fall under the cross
And graze his knees.

Should I not then cry, *Mercy?*

Lighten our darkness

When I was a child,
They were killing children
And I didn't know;
Men and women too,
Led to the gas chambers
By people who were
Only obeying orders.

Now I am grown, aware;
It happens still, not always
By deliberate act –
A terrible carelessness
Corrupts our use of power,
Lets people be expendable.

I can't blame 'them';
Like everyone, I have within
A place of guilt and shame,
Like Auschwitz, where
It's always night.

With you, Lord,
Darkness is light.
Strengthen your light in us
Until it snuffs out darkness.

Elie Wiesel, an Auschwitz survivor, speaking at a ceremony commemorating the fiftieth anniversary of the discoveries at Auschwitz, said, 'Here it is always night.' People at that ceremony lit candles and placed them on the railway tracks leading to the gas chambers. The event coincided with Candlemas.

Uphill journey

I've always lived on the edge of a map:
Hints about what lies around, but
No clear topography. Perhaps,
If I'd known about the
Arduous contours,
Choosing another route,
I'd have missed also
The breathtaking beauty.

Life style

Deny yourself, but first
Establish who you are.
He surely did not mean
We must deny our gifts,
Make ourselves nothing.
Premature self-denial
Ends in stunted growth;
What's needed is not
Self-negation, but, springing from
Self-awareness, generous
Giving, not up, but out.

Only human

'You must be perfect' awoke
Echoes from somewhere –
'Be a good girl, or else ...'
And once again I thought
'I'll never manage it.'

But does perfection come
Through striving to attain
Imposed, impossible standards,
Hard-edged flawlessness?

Deep down I feel
The opposite is true:
Perfection comes
Through gentleness,
Loving hurts to wholeness,
Growing to be at ease
With self and God.

Terminology

Productivity:
Forced outcome of
Endeavour;

Unlike *fruitfulness:*
Result of fallow
Darkness
When time seems wasted.

Seasons take their time:
Nothing is lost, our waiting,
Open and expectant
Leads to harvest.

Goddisgoode

Written like God's
E-mail address,
In years gone by
It was the name for yeast,
Mysterious, powerful,
Whose origin, like Manna's
No one knew. And so
They called it *goddisgoode*
Because, they said,
It cometh of the grece of Godde.

That is the heart of all.

What's in a word?

Present, a mean word
To describe an offering.

Presents come from
A position of strength –
You have something to give.
An *offering* comes from
Weakness, an opening of
Yourself in vulnerability –
A handful of wilting flowers
Clutched by a child, offered
'For you'.
Always inadequate,
But received and valued.

The last verse of 'When I survey the wondrous cross'
has variant readings:

Were the whole realm of nature mine,
That were ⎰ *a present far too small*
⎱ *an offering*
Love so amazing, so divine,
Demands my soul, my life, my all.

Poor young man

'Get rid of it,' he said, 'and follow me.'
I wish I could.
Wealth alienates me from my fellows,
Both by their envy and through my
Preoccupations. It's such a weight,
I'd love to lose the burden.
But the power that goes with wealth,
Could I lose that? Throw in my lot
With those who follow him, with
Nothing to my name, no guarantees of
Home or friends, or favour?
It's such a lot to ask, too much to lose.
And yet, I'm haunted by his look.
Others who've asked me to give up my
Wealth have held out grasping hands
To ease it from me. But he looked at me
As though he understood just what it
Meant: no easy gesture, but complete
Upheaval of my life. And when I
Turned to go, he did not blame, but
Loved me still. He haunts me ...
Can I forego the riches of that love?
Can I let my wealth go?

Mark 10.17-22

Small boy

I only had five loaves and
Two small fish. Barely enough for me,
Let alone all that crowd.
And when he said he wanted them,
I laughed. Feed all those thousands
With my food? Go on!
But, as I watched, he did.
He took it, blessed it,
Broke it, shared,
And they were fed.
They even had leftovers.
He was great.
It wasn't magic, but
A greater power that
Made me think that
He could feed the world.
When I grow up,
I'm going to follow him!

John 6.9

Fragment

Feed on him in your heart, digest his power;
Let his life slow-release itself into your blood,
Stream through your senses, energise your thought.
Recall his presence thankfully,
A constant savouring.

Zacchaeus

I walk tall now.
After those years of
Having to make my mark
Fair means or foul,
I know myself valued.
Elbowed out of the way,
Forced to assert myself
The only way I knew,
By getting rich at your
Expense, even having to
Climb a tree because
You wouldn't let me see ...

And then, he saw me,
Looked and saw me,
Scared that my littleness
Would keep me down.
He looked and said,
'It's you I want,
Come down and let me
Join you at your house.'

Me!

And now, I'll never be the same again.
From now on I can look you in the eye.
I'll give back all I took unfairly,
What's more, I'll give it back four-fold.
And all because he looked at me and
Saw me, and loved me as I was and
As I am.

I walk tall now.

Luke 19.1-10

Caught in the act

I waited for the stones to
Cut my flesh, sharp pointed
Thrusts of angry scorn
Purging my accusers of their
Guilt. But one by one they
Left, themselves accused by
His sharp questioning,
'Who among you is sinless?'

I stood alone,
Waiting to be condemned, but
As he looked, knowing me as I am,
Love set me free,
To go and sin no more.

John 8.3-11

Second Commandment

Love your neighbour as yourself.
The trouble is, we do.
And since we do not always love ourselves,
Our neighbour suffers from our handicap.
Strange feelings come from depths we don't
Control, causing us to react, and not respond.

How can we learn to love our dark unknown,
Embrace, accept, forgive what lies within?

Can we believe it is already done?
We are profoundly loved, both in our depths
And to the limit of his love, which has no end.
A starting place, with time and then eternity
To learn its truth. And, in the meantime,
What a blessing for our neighbour, to be
Loved as we (are learning to) love ourselves.

Martha

Maligned through much of history for being
Over active, missing the better part.
Alternatively, praised for keeping the show going.
After all, people have to eat.

But practical concerns did not preclude you
From discernment, even if at times
They got you down. Intuitive, assertive,
You spoke your mind, and things got done.
Lazarus was raised, the meals prepared,
All kept in order.

A woman loved and valued, not for meekness
But awareness. You were the first to hear
'I am the Resurrection and the Life.' And
Your response, 'You are the Christ', has
Echoed down the ages, encouraging those
Whom some would confine to the kitchen
To share their insights, not with aggression,
But with the certainty that
Women can be right.

Too busy to pray

It must have smarted,
That implied rebuke.*
She was only doing
What hospitality required,
And they would both
Want to be fed.

But when she thought about it later,
I wonder if she realised
She too had a choice?

She could have sat with Mary at his feet
Absorbed in his teaching,
Enlarging her inner space;
Work would have waited.

Perhaps then Mary would have
Joined her in the chores,
And both discovered
The better part that
None can take away,
Their work transformed
By the presence
They had practised.

* Luke 10.38-42

No easy place

In this room, where you can see
The city through one window,
The cathedral through another
(Mary and Martha as it were, opposed)
The question comes again,
Where do we find you?

The dominant building
Makes assumptions not borne out
By experience, for
Bruised and broken people
Live in both aspects, and
Prayer is made in busy streets
As well as cathedral calm.

God, elusive, slips
Out of the fortress
Built to keep him safe, and
Wanders the streets, looking for
Allies willing to try
The steep hill of connection,
And keep him company
In work and prayer, without
Prescribing the location.

Written in Edward King House, Lincoln, in the room Bishop King referred to as the Mary and Martha room. The hill joining the cathedral and castle to the rest of the city is called, and is, Steep Hill.

Movable feast?

How do you feel, Thomas,
Your day being moved
From winter solstice
To high holiday?

Perhaps you rejoice in
More attention, away from
The tinselled run-up to
The Christmas Feast.
For me, reflection on
Faith emerging from doubt,
The stirring of meaning,
Needs darker symbols:
Has more to do with
The almost imperceptible
Shift of the earth on its axis,
A flicker of light
On the shortest
Day,
Than a blaze of certainty
In midsummer's sun.

St Thomas the Apostle: observed in Book of Common Prayer *calendar on 21 December, in* Common Worship *calendar on 3 July.*

Known by name

Who were you, Mary
From whom devils were cast out?
Did you disturb respectability
By washing his feet with tears,
An uninvited guest;
Or in embarrassing extravagance
Pour precious ointment on his head?
Were you notorious in your day,
Or a woman in the crowd from Magdala,
Who found new purpose
Being set free to love,
And used your gifts
In faithful ministry?

Perhaps it doesn't matter.
Perhaps, like all of us,
You were a mixture:
Damaged and healed;
Longing to be loved,
And struggling to relate;
Passionate and reserved
By turns, working out
Costly discipleship.

The important moment
Was when you heard your name,
And answered and were sent,
No longer clinging to what kept you safe,
Strong in the power of the risen Lord,
To witness to new life.

Mary of Magdala

A nudge and a wink your assessment.
It has suited men so.
To admit to alternatives
Would be too upsetting.
Yet consider the evidence:
Healed of an illness unspecified,
(Subject of much speculation);
Named first of the women
Whose ministry nourished and cared for him;
Leader, a force to be reckoned with;
Love marked by faithfulness,
Courage too, there at the Cross.
First of the witnesses,
You met the risen Lord,
You were sent first with the News,
Meeting incredulous men,
Who dismissed you
As bearer of women's tales.

From that day onward, women have
Shown they have insight:
Men have been slow to believe.

Dinner Party

Simon

I'll do the decent thing,
Invite him for a meal.
I needn't make a fuss,
He should feel honoured to be
Here. No need to lavish
Courtesy on him.
Master, you're welcome,
Seat yourself, enjoy
The food and company.

Woman

How can he treat him so?
If Simon knew
What kind of man he is
He'd not dismiss him
So discourteously.
Master, with my tears,
And perfume once
Used to my shame,
I'll wash your feet
In loving gratitude.

Other guests

What's going on? That harlot
Drawing attention to herself!
She ought to know
We don't want her sort here,
Flaunting extravagant
Emotion. And he says
Her sins have been forgiven.
What's going on?

Jesus

Simon, what motivates your 'love'?
Desire to be thought well of? Or
Response in gratitude for sins
Forgiven? This woman knows.
Daughter, your faith has saved you.
Go in peace.

Luke 7.36-50

Elder brother

'All that I have is yours,'
He said. But I was so angry
That I could not hear him.
All that fuss about my wastrel
Brother, coming home begging
When he'd had his fun;
Throwing a party for him,
After his extravagance with
Women, travel, living like a lord;
While I've been stuck here,
Slogging my guts out,
Earning my half share.
Did he really think I'd
Welcome his return,
A rival to the inheritance?
He's had his share.

But that's just what Dad said:
All that he has is mine.
There's no injustice, only
My feeling that it isn't fair.
But can I say that I was better?
More dutiful perhaps, but loving?
I've never said to Dad,
'I need you', or let him show
How much he needed me.
Perhaps I hurt him just as much
By staying in grudging service, as
My brother did by seeming not to care.
Perhaps we've never had a party
Because I've always been so far away.

And now he's found me,
Asked me with tenderness
To share the feast.

I'll go and say to him, 'I'm sorry,
Can I come home, and be your son?'

Luke 15.25-32

Simon of Cyrene

It wasn't what I'd planned –
My pilgrimage to join the Passover
Ended cross-carrying, glad
My sons weren't witness to my shame.

But the man, bleeding in pain –
His dignity impressed: no cursing,
But forgiving words absorbing cruelty.
Although I had the cross, it seemed
He had the weight, almost as though
World's pain bore down on him.
What should be memory of shame,
Stays with me as a turning point in love;
I felt compelled to go not just a mile,
But on an endless journey into life.

Mark 15.21

Alexander and Rufus

They pressed him into carrying a cross,
And he was changed. Instead of feeling shame,
He said he'd glory always in that sign.
Impressed, we also turned, confessed Christ Lord,
And bear his mark of love.

St Anne

The moment every mother dreads:
Whatever did you feel like?
Could you share it with your
Husband? Did you feel, like
Joseph, that there was no
Alternative to putting her
Away privily? Even then
There was the rest of the family,
And the neighbours were bound to talk.
The shame of it.

Gracious, your name means.
You must have been a real
Source of grace to Mary,
Supporting her through those months.
One of those people
Who make it possible
For others to cope.

Man of fire *(St Francis)*

We've turned him into someone
Who was kind to animals,
Drowned him in sentiment.

But this man was impossible:
An all or nothing man
With fire in his belly.
He gave up all, that
Nothing should
Stand in the way of
Absolute commitment.

Of course he was kind,
And full of respect for
All creation. Perhaps
He recognised in animals
His own directness.

But he was uncomfortable too;
He stripped life of
Pretensions to power,
Insisted that we should
Embrace the leper of
Our own unloveliness,
And live out love
In great simplicity.

Cloud of witnesses

What if time is not a continuous line,
But a series of concentric circles.
Then human life would not be,
As for Bede's sparrow,* a matter of
Flying into the light for a brief period
On a long migration from darkness to
Darkness. More like an appearance
In a vast arena, where all the actors
Play their part under the brilliant lights,
Then fade into the auditorium, beyond the glare,
Making space for new arrivals.
We laugh and love, and struggle to make sense of
Half a script, finding the writing
Difficult to read, frustrated in our effort
By the inability of others
To get their lines right, or their sheer
Obstructiveness; ad-libbing our way
Out of difficult situations,
Rejoicing when all goes well.
And all around us, those who
Have had their turn, or
Wait in trepidation for their cue,
Watch, supporting us with sympathetic
Tears or laughter, urging us on
In loving fellowship.

Then, when the play is over,
And the lights go up,
We shall meet them, and have time,
Or will it be eternity, to enjoy
Their company. Time too to meet the Author,
And discuss our part, learning the value of
Our contribution, which had never been in doubt
In his mind, only in our faltering confidence.

Bede, in his 'Ecclesiastical History of the English Nation', records the discussion King Edwin held with his courtiers about the possibility of adopting the Christian Faith. One of his advisers said that life seemed to be like the flight of a sparrow through the feasting hall in winter. While the bird is in the hall, it is safe from the storms outside, but then it vanishes again into the darkness from which it came, and no one knows what becomes of it. He said that if the new faith held any clues to the uncertainties surrounding our earthly life, it should be given serious consideration.

Ashing

Light as a feather
A finger touched me,
Branded me cross-shaped,
Smudged me with ash.

Light as a feather,
God's finger caressed me
With sign of forgiveness,
Marked me with love.

Light as a feather,
Penitent, shriven,
Signed with his life-mark,
I go on my way.

Lent

Lent is a time to learn to travel
Light, to clear the clutter
From our crowded lives, and
Find a space, a desert.
Deserts are bleak: no creature
Comforts, only a vast expanse of
Stillness, sharpening awareness of
Ourselves and God.

Uncomfortable places, deserts.

Most of the time we're tempted to
Avoid them, finding good reasons to
Live lives of ease; cushioned by
Noise from self-discovery,
Clutching at world's success
To stave off fear.
But if we dare to trust the silence
To strip away our false security,
God can begin to grow his wholeness in us,
Fill up our emptiness, destroy our fears,
Give us new vision, courage for the journey,
And make our desert blossom like a rose.

Maundy Thursday

What, let you wash my feet?
Shouldn't it be the other way,
Me kneeling before you?
I don't think I can take such
Personal service – feet are
Funny things, shaped by experience,
Calloused and blistered;
I'm half ashamed to show
The state they're in.
And you might tickle,
I'd be helpless, at your mercy.

But you're serious, aren't you.
If I refuse, you say, I don't belong.
Take me then, Lord, and plunge me in,
Not just my feet, but everything.

Why are you laughing? Too
Extravagant? Trusting you with my
Feet would be enough?
I want to do more than test the water,
I want to jump in with both ... Oh,
I see ... Lord, I am slow.

Please, wash my feet.

John 13.1-11

Challenge

On that night, there were
Two bowls of water.

The first was taken
And used for washing feet,
Symbol, he said, of love.

The second was called for
And used for washing hands,
Disclaiming responsibility.

The bowls are constantly before us:
Into which will we dip our hands?

Shades of despair

Pilate

If only they would stop that
Shouting, 'Caesar's friend,
You are not Caesar's friend
If you let this man go.' He's
Innocent, I find no fault, but
They insist. His life or mine, it seems.
'Not Caesar's friend' leads only to one
End. Who is this man? 'Behold him!'
'Crucify!' 'I wash my hands ...'
'His blood on us,' they cry.
And as they lead him out,
My blood runs cold.

Judas

I thought he'd fight, I thought
He would at last admit that
I was right, the only way to
Win Messiah's cause was by the
Sword. He should have acted
When they yelled, 'Save now!'
He could have overthrown them.
I was wrong. My treacherous kiss
Condemned both him and me:
Him to a cross, and me to
Death of hope. My only course now
Is to end it all.

Peter

What have I done? I who would
Never leave him, so I said.
What have I done? I slept
When he most needed company,
Denied I knew him when he
Needed friends, ran when
They led him to a cross,
Stayed distant in his suffering.
How can I bear the memory of his look,
The love accepting me as friend?
Master, what have I done?

Crossroads *(The Centurion at the Crucifixion)*

I cursed my luck, on duty in that heat:
The flies, the blood, the stench of death.
It was the loneliest place I've ever known,
Standing beside that cross. The crowds
Hurling abuse engulfed me with their hate;
Had he no friends? Standing not far away,
The women had more courage than the men,
But even his God, it seemed, had left him.
I've seen some crucifixions in my time,
But never one like this: the victim
More concerned for others than himself,
Asking forgiveness for his murderers.
And then that aweful darkness, when the
World died with him, and the cry that
Pierced the darkness pierced me too.
Did he say, 'Finished'? The way I feel,
It's only just begun.

Rood-tree

I might have been his cradle,
Rocking him, folding
Securely against harm.
I could have been a ship,
Turning my sturdy timbers
To the wind, keeping him
Safe from storm.

Instead, they used me as
His cross.

No infant rages rocked the
Cradle tree, or storm lashed ship
Such as unleashed on me
That day. Shock waves of hatred
Crashed against me, bearing
On me through his body
Weight of world's pain,
Weight of his agony;
Wringing from him
Drop by drop,
'Why, God, you too?'

No comforting protection
Could I offer, or deliverance;
Only support, his mainstay in distress.

But did I hold him, or did he
With strength of purpose lovingly
Embrace his work of suffering,
Stretched on my arms?

They say it was a tree whose fruit
Brought sorrow to the world.
The fruit I bore,
Though seeming shame,
They call salvation.

My glory was it then,
To be his tree.

Easter Morning

Do not cling …
Let me be bigger than your
Heart can hold.
Rise with me to a
Larger vision.

Emmaus walk

'Don't talk to strangers,' we are
Told in childhood. It takes years
To grow through infant training.
Daring to trust comes with maturity,
Or perhaps is born of desperation.
The Emmaus two discovered
That the stranger unlocked
Understanding;
Shared food became a blessing.

Luke 24.13-35

Easter

In the beginning
The Lord God planted a garden
Facing the rising sun.
Adam was the gardener,
And all was very good
Until, worming its way
Into his mind the idea
Came that he could
Do things his way.

And the rest was trouble.

But in another garden,
The risen Son, Adam renewed
Appearing as a gardener
Brought new beginning,
Showed that through God's grace
All can be life.

Restoration

Master, don't tease. You know
I am your friend. Yet still you ask,
And how can I reply?
I swore unending loyalty, and then
Three times denied, but Lord,
I am your friend. And still you press,
You are my friend, then? Lord it hurts,
But in the hurting heals:
Three times I say it, Yes, I am your friend.
And gladly I will serve as you command.

John 21.15-17

Perspective

Ascension means a
God-like view of things,
Rising above our usual
Limitations.
Rise, then, and know
The glory of a life
Set free from fear.

Wait for the Spirit

Wait ...
Without expectation
Which might focus
Attention too narrowly,
So that we miss the coming.

Wait with expectancy, alert,
Hearts, minds, hands, ears
Open to receive the gift.

Lord, have mercy

God, you overstepped the mark
At Pentecost. Those boundaries
So clearly drawn: be clean,
Be holy, do not dare draw near
Unless your hearts are pure,
Your sins forgiven – they kept us safe.
Then suddenly, with burning fire
And rushing wind,
You broke down our defences,
Surprised your way
Into our lives.

We're at your mercy.
Can we bear
To be that close?

Exodus 19.10-12
Acts 2.1-4

Jeu d'esprit

Flame-dancing Spirit, come,
Sweep us off our feet and
Dance us through our days.
Surprise us with your rhythms,
Dare us to try new steps, explore
New patterns and new partnerships.
Release us from old routines,
To swing in abandoned joy
And fearful adventure.
And in the intervals,
Rest us,
In your still centre.

Trinity

Father, Son and Holy Spirit,
Mother, Daughter, He and She,
Compassed in one mystery.
Pattern of all relationships,
Creating, powerful;
Sustaining, not contained,
Outflowing into us
Drawn into you. O Holy God
We worship you.

Unless a seed dies

Christ is in me, the life
Within the seed-case of my self,
Waiting to be set free.
Light growing in darkness,
In secret, patiently
Pushing against self-will.

Christ is the secret that
I cannot keep, he will
Break through entombing
Fearfulness; my seed-case
Broken open will release
His life, his image
Forming my maturity.

Transfiguration

A moment of blinding perception –
It would be good to stay there,
But clutch it, and it's gone.
They come unheralded,
Those moments of dazzling clarity,
And leave us as suddenly.

As well try catch the kingfisher
Darting through stillness.

Be thankful for its jewelled beauty,
And keep awake, alert.

Thoughts on August 6th

Bright light around him
Transfiguring with glory;
Giving us insight.

Harsh light above us,
Mushroom-shaped cloud destroying
Hope for the future.

Soft light of candles
Sent on their way by peace-folk;
Pushing back darkness.

Giving us insight,
Hope for the future,
Pushing back darkness.

6 August is the day in the Church calendar when the Transfiguration of Christ (Mark 9.2-8) is remembered. It is also the day on which the bomb was dropped on Hiroshima. Many groups of people throughout the world float lighted candles in paper boats on rivers and lakes on this day, as a sign of sorrow for the devastation caused to human life, and as an act of dedication to peace.

Power games

When we play God
We throw our weight around,
Treat people like chess pieces,
Play our game regardless of their
Gifts. Their value lies in
Cost-effectiveness, not in
Intrinsic worth. And if we lose,
We simply change the rules
And use them to our own advantage.

Lord, it must sometimes
Break your heart, to see how
We mismanage your creation,
Misuse freedom. Are you sometimes
Tempted to break our teeth,
Hurl thunderbolts, cry
Halt?

It must be most
Frustrating
Being
God.

Not the last word

It feels as though all that I've given
Is being thrown back in my teeth.
Those years of effort, care and dedication
Evaluated in that one chill word,
Redundant.
But though they have decided
They can do without me,
I do not accept the label, failure.
My value does not lie in cost-effectiveness
But in experience, skills, talents;
I am me.

I'm not redundant, I'm available.

I hope to God that's true.
Right now I feel as though
I'm at the crucifixion,
Crying in agony
Why have you let me down?
There were no guarantees then,
Were there, that there would be
Resurrection.

Bed and breakfast

I live sheltered by the name
For a cheap holiday.
Some holiday. A family of slugs
Lives in the bathroom, mice scurry
Grey as fear. There is the occasional
Rat. But what I mind most is being
Squashed with the children in one room,
Loving, fighting, eating, sleeping
Publicly; queueing to use facilities
Stained by others' existence.
So, I have a roof. Must I be always
Thankful for small mercies?
What I want is a home.
Sod your trickle down economy,
The only thing that trickles here is
Rain, relentlessly through the ceiling.
Trickle, God, can't you send a flood,
Justice in torrents to carry me to my
Dream home? Nothing elaborate: just
Damp-free, no fungus in the corners;
The only creatures there present by
Invitation; water running through pipes;
Space, privacy. Not much to ask.

Missed childhood

I was no latch-key kid,
We had no home.
Each day we left
The place we'd slept in,
Plastic bags holding our
Treasures, and we walked,
A leisured class,
Hopelessly killing time.
We looked at shops, and
Sat in parks, and
Waited to go inside.
I couldn't watch my mum
To learn her skills,
There was no space for
Creativity. I learnt
Survival,
Living's another thing.

Acceptable losses?

The men on the screen
Use language that cleans up war;
Talk of surgical precision
Taking out enemy power,
Leave unseen the effects
Of the not-so-smart weapons:
The homes being bombed,
The fear and the deaths and the maiming.
They assure us, unwilling voyeurs,
That our side is performing to plan.
Ours? Who asked us to join?
We are caught, like the cormorants
Oiled with our evil,
Reluctant participants in war.

Lament

The weight of the tears of the world
Is too heavy to bear:
For the cost, and the waste of
Young lives playing out
Old men's games,
Knowing terror and fear
Never tasted by soldiers of lead.

Forgive us, I fear
That we know very well
What we do.

Written during the Gulf War, 1991.

Asylum seekers

They live under the shadow of
A two-edged sword: in a place of safety
And a state of fear. The rules
Ensure *we* are kept safe; *our* fear
Defines our hospitality,
Keeps them on edge.
Compassion is constrained
By prudent care.

Could we, instead of seeing problems,
Begin to recognise the gifts they bring,
And be enriched by their humanity?

Refugees

They stream across our screens
Balancing impossible burdens;
The remnants of their lives
Tied up in bundles.
Yet what we see is nothing
To the burden they carry
In their hearts:
Loss, pain and fear.

Temple cleansing

Sometimes the only right response is
Anger. Not dull resentment,
Poisoning all it touches, or
Bitterness that taints the memory,
But a clean cutting edge, that
Lances festering grievances,
Releasing energy to fight;
The fuel of passion that
Challenges evils,
Outwardly observed
Or known within.

Such anger is not sin.

De profundis

How long, O Lord, how long?
A silly question.

Do you, beyond the tick of time,
For whom a thousand years
Flash like an evening,
Do you know how it feels
When evenings, days, months
Drag, a thousand years?
The seeming endlessness of care,
Commitment carrying on
Long after energy is spent,
Do you, who slumber not
Know that bone-weariness?

'My strength sufficient.' Yes,
I hear you, Lord. My head
Acknowledges that you are right.
The question in my guts is,
'Is it true? Can I hang on
Until your timelessness
Pervades my life, and
Makes the question meaningless?'

Mothercare

Mother and child

I wonder what you are thinking as you sit there.
Are you remembering how you washed the
Child you bore? These hands, so
Frail and gnarled now, washed and
Gentled me. Now I wash you.
Your feet, so painful sometimes,
Carried you on endless journeys of caring;
Kneeling to wash them is an act of homage.
Are you remembering how when you were young
You pleased yourself about what you wore, and
Where you went? Now another puts your clothes
     ready,
And guides your unsteady steps.
Who is the child now, who the mother?
Do you remember sitting as I do,
Torn between wanting to help, and needing to
Leave dignity and independence free? Was it
A kind of death to you, that to be free,
I had to grow away? Your freedom now
Can only come through death, a
Painful letting go for both of us.

We'll never talk about these things,
But sometimes, when I tuck you into bed,
You look at me with impish humour,
As though you know what I am thinking,
Child, mother.

Mother

My brain, why won't it work?
When what's-her-name,
The person looking after me,
Asks what I'd like for tea,
The choices slither out of reach
And I don't know.
Dressing's another thing:
Those clothes, I used to
Put them on in seconds,
Now I can't remember how to do it,
And sometimes go downstairs
Without my dress. You'd think
I'd realise – I feel such a fool.
My memory – ask me what happened when
Scott reached Antarctica, and I can tell you
How I read about it to the school, best
Reader of them all. But ask me
What I've had for dinner, and
I can't remember. Have I had my dinner?

They take me out, that's good.
We watch the sea, and laugh at people
Falling off those boards;
Or go where there are animals, they know
I love to see the newborn ones.
I store up all my news to tell
Whoever hasn't taken me,
But when we meet, I can't remember,
And tell them anything to cover up
This muddle in my head.
But we all know it isn't right.

I've lived too long. They're very kind,
And say it isn't true. But really we all know.

'Ah, hello dear, I hoped you'd come.
I want to tell you – what was it?'

Daughter

Dear Mum, she gets so muddled,
Such a shame. She loses things –
We never found her teeth –
Or hides them. Was there a childhood
Prohibition about food being left on plates?
That would explain leftovers hidden
In the pot she puts her teeth in
When she's tired of wearing them.
A nice surprise for whoever cleans her teeth,
The new ones, that is. I hate false teeth,
And that pot. Neither will survive her long!
Those men who wake her early in the morning,
Clearing the snow (improbable in June)
Or pumping water, who are they? 'They're
Something at the College,' she says
Knowingly. And all those crowds of people
Who go past at night, invisible to us –
'A special meeting somewhere, about
Something,' – she always knows.
'What's today? Then where did Monday go?
Tomorrow I shall only have two pills.
I always know it's Wednesday by the pills.'
But tomorrow she'll say, 'Only two? Why's that?'

It's been a busy day, the gasman called,
Hardly disturbing the tedium of her time.
She who bore children, ran a home,
Rarely sat idle, can't remember that,
Looks blankly at a picture of her husband
Married to her more than fifty years.
Then mother's instinct surfaces,
She puts the kettle on for tea.

A burnt dry kettle has a special smell –
We always have a spare now, just in case.
At least the gas lit this time ...
'I thought there was a funny smell,' she says.
Dear Mum.

Still growing

My mother died some time ago.
The person I now care for,
Though she looks the same,
Has lost her power.
No longer archetypal,
Giver of life, solver of problems,
Source of wisdom, but
A frail old lady, confused and
Almost past the stage of knowing it.
(Though suddenly the other night
She said, 'Old age defeats me,
Who'd have thought that I'd go
Funny in the head like this?')

Watching her tears me inwardly.
Why should she suffer this disintegration,
Going on wearily from day to day?

Yet in her waiting there is hope.
Delightful still in personality,
She grows serenely on to her next stage.
Faltering strength and ceasing to be mother
Are staging posts, not ends, for her.
She's waiting in anticipation for her next
Adventure. 'When the time is right,' she says,
'I'll go.'

Identity crisis

A nightied figure on the stairs
The second time that evening,
'I can't sleep.'
Once more I led my mother back to bed.
'Sleep well,' I said, 'I'll soon be up myself.'
'Don't disturb Ann,' she said maternally.
'I won't,' said Ann.

Second childhood

We sit and watch the sky change,
And she tells me how she used to sit
In childhood at the farm, and
Watch the sunset, glorious colours
Streaking the horizon.
And now a second childhood,
Cruel in reversal.
No growth to independence, as
One by one abilities are lost.
Sleep is not now renewal, only a
Respite from dulled sense and memory.
Frustration, once alleviated by
Mastery of skills, increases as the
Need for help grows greater, personal
Freedom less. Life goes full circle,
Death a second birth.

Life cycle

All birth is dying, a
Painful struggle to emerge
From the imprisoning womb,
Weary of growing in darkness;
The longing, shared by
Mother and child, through
Pain of parturition to be
Given new opportunities to love.

Then is death, bearing fruit,
Matched by an equal struggle to be
Free of the imprisoning body,
Separated from the cords of love
Which bind us to each other,
Proving at last to be
Constraints on growth?

Now as I let her go,
As she once gave me birth,
I feel the birth pangs of
My mother's death.

A time to mourn

I have been years grieving
Many little deaths:
Loss of mother, as
The roles reversed and
I became her carer;
Loss of recognition, as
Generations mingled and I
Found myself her mother, sister,
Or, more painful, stranger;
Loss of reference points,
As times and seasons merged
Into long twilight.

And now, her care entrusted
To the hands of others,
Loss of shared experience
Leaves me at a loss.

Ad quem

Death – terminus,
Heart-stopping jolt
At the end of the line?
Or junction, where worlds meet,
Faith catching the connection?

Farewells

I always hated those times at the station,
When, goodbyes said, we found ourselves
Locked into meaningless chatter or
Awkward silences, as the train
Waited for its signal.
What could we say? No conversation
Could be guaranteed completion.
Pain of parting
Smarted behind the eyelids,
As we struggled to be cheerful.

Waiting as life draws to its close
Can be like that. Longing for release,
But dreading the moment of departure.

Death

I visited each day
To see if she was there;
To catch a flicker of response,
A smile. But she was gone,
Lingering in another place
Until her unresponsive body
Could catch up with dying.
A winter of waiting, then
Just at the greening of the spring,
Released, she died.

I do not weep for her,
Born to new life;
The tears I shed are for myself,
An adult who has lost a friend,
A child her mother.

Tide-turn

Grief.
Desolate emptiness;
A muddy estuary
Haunted with
Melancholy cries.

A year on,
And imperceptibly
The channels have
Filled with water.

Sunlight dances.

My spirit,
Stirring with the shifting tide,
Takes up the journey.

Compassion

Suffering, sharing
The pain;
Knowing within oneself
Some of the cost.
Spurred to activity,
One hand stretched out
To those who suffer,
One stretched out to
God who suffers too.
Nothing sentimental:
The sharp edge of love,
Like crucifixion.

Bereavement

Dark place
Where, vulnerable, alone,
We lick the wounds of loss.

Wise friends say little,
But hold us in their love,
And listen.

There are no guarantees,
Only reports from those
Who've been there,
That there is hope,
And life persists.

Tomb

The place of remembering:
Where as the work of grief is done,
Memory recovers its perspective.

Letting the dead one go,
With aching sense of loss,
Opens the way to finding again
A rounded person, gifts and faults
Delights and irritations;
Makes it possible to share again
The jokes, the intimate glance,
Keep company unseen.

Resurrection

There are times when,
All being darkness and loss,
There is nothing for it
But to pick up your cross
And dance with it.

Preparation

From sudden death,
Good Lord, deliver us.

But death is always sudden,
Slipping between one moment
And eternity. We can't escape.
Indeed, that way of death
Is what I hope for:
Not for me the painful diminishment
Of long, slow dying –
That's much more to be feared.

The trouble is, that
When death suddenly
Catches our breath
We leave loose ends,
Relationships at odds
Or words unsaid:
Fuel for guilt for those
Surviving, quite apart
From any personal
Dissatisfaction.

Perhaps our prayer should be
For more awareness;
Not preoccupation
With our mortal end,
But aliveness to
This moment's possibilities.
It may just be our last.

For sudden death,
Good Lord, prepare us.

Autumn

After a sharp frost, on a windless morning,
I watched leaves falling ...

The frost has made the leaves
Lose their grip. Like pattering rain
They fall, returning to earth.

Might death be like that,
A gentle falling to the dust
From which I came?
Must I go raging into that
Dark night? Could I not,
As the sharp frost of age
Begins to chill,
Simply let go?

Year's mind

Every year, I pass the day
Not knowing. Someday
Someone will say, 'Oh yes,
Ann died a year ago.'

I pray they will remember
A day when I lived to the full,
A day of celebration
Of the gift of life.

Last Things

Death

It is not death I fear, but
Dying. How will it come?
Will it be sudden, violent,
Catching me in surprise or
Indignation? Or a slow
Decline, stripping away
Control, perhaps with pain or
Loss of faculties? Those I fear.
Could I choose, I would go gently,
Full of years, to that still place
Where flesh and spirit part.
Travelling light, as when I first
Arrived, naked, to birth.

Judgement

Death is a gift, God's last,
Perhaps his greatest,
Setting us free to know him
As he is, and see ourselves
Uncluttered by our outward
Circumstance. And then,
Our motives bared before us,
Will we stand,
Looking God in the eye, gladly
Acknowledging our inmost selves?
Or will we understand at last
Why we pray, 'Lord, have mercy'?

Hell

It would be hell to find
It was a lie, this talk of
God. To meet not him, but
Emptiness. No need for
Torment, flaming fire, the
Medieval tortures:
To wake and find there's
Nothing would be Hell.

Heaven

How can our language,
Formed for time and space, express
The timeless graciousness of God?
What of ourselves, how will we be
When limits to loving are removed?
To know how we are known,
The judgement past, should fill us
Not with terror but with joy.
Complete acceptance in the love of God –
Will that be Heaven?

Special

There was always the chance
That I wouldn't be picked;
Standing there as the best friends
And the good at games were called,
Fear that I'd be left, not chosen, but
Taken because there was no one else.
The shame of it.

And later, a different game,
Where the hurts were deeper,
As groups paired into couples,
And I, not chosen or choosing,
Remained, the encouraging,
'Your turn next', ringing
Ever more hollow.

I'm a long time learning
How deeply I'm valued;
God-chosen and cherished
(Which doesn't deny the aloneness)
I'm set free to love in my turn.

Single bliss

'It's easier for you,' they said,
'Having no family.'
They mean, of course, I'm free, not cluttered up
With other people's problems.
My house, once tidied, stays that way,
Without the trail of toys and cast-off
Clothing up the stairs, the muddy footmarks
And the tide-marked bath.
Food's left for its intended purpose, not
Picked at by impatient hands, or
Prematurely eaten.

If that is what life's for, it's easier.
But outward order does not bring content.
Realities of life lie in relationships,
And at the heart of singleness one is
Alone.
Of course, the barren women do keep house,*
No one will do it for them. But to be a
Joyful mother, one always has to borrow
Someone else's children.

*Psalm 113.8.

Half the story

Male and female he created them.
Suppose that doesn't mean that
Neither is complete without the other,
But that no one is complete, until
The two are recognised and reconciled within?

If the quest is not so much to find
Completion in another, but fulfilment
In one's own integrity, then
Being single is not condemnation,
A yin for ever searching for its yang,
But opportunity to grow in inner wholeness,
Without distraction of another's pain.
A lonelier path, but just as capable
Of leading to maturity in love.

Not at all

'More blessed to give than to receive,'
You said. You could have added 'easier'.
Why do we back away from compliments?
Why not with proper pride receive
Due recognition of our gifts?
In undervaluing ourselves,
We do scant honour to the one
Whose gifts we are.

A hug

How good it is being held,
Not clutched, exploited or possessed,
But held, delighted in,
Strength flowing each to each,
Rejoicing in each other's company.

Change

My body needs to mourn its
Childlessness; the bloody
Waste, and pain that brought forth
Nothing.
Caressed and cradled by
Fresh understanding,
To reaffirm
Creativeness.

Celtic knot

The tangled roots from which I spring
Nourish my depths and
Send out shoots for growth;
Separate yet entwined
Friends, relatives, strangers
And people I don't like,
We grow together in
Intricate relationship.

Weaver God, pick up the
Threads of my experience,
Craft the pattern, and
In your time
Reveal significance.

Life blessing

Deep peace enfold you,
Encircle and hold you
In youth and in age,
At life's every stage.
At birth and in growing,
In failing and dying,
The sacred three
Your protection be.

Age blessing

At ear close and tooth drop,
At sight fail and mind loss,
The sacred three
Enliven thee.

Lullaby

Rest in the love of the Father,
Rest in the love of the Son,
Rest in the love of the Spirit.
The love of the sacred Three
Your rest-place be.

Revelation

God's work of art.
That's me?
Then beauty must lie
In the eye of the
Beholder.

I feel more like
One of those statues
Michelangelo left
Half emerging
From the marble block;
Full of potential,
On the verge of life,
But prisoned still
By circumstance and
Fear.

Yet part of me is free –
And you are still creating,
Bringing to life
The promise that is there.
Sometimes by
Hammer blows
Which jar my being,
Sometimes by
Tender strokes half felt
Which waken me to
Life.

Go on, Lord.
Love me into wholeness.
Set me free
To share with you
In your creative joy;
To laugh with you
At your delight
In me,
Your work of art.

After Word

Thus heavens and earth were
Finished, and were good. But
In the middle of the night, God woke.
'It might be burdensome,' he thought,
'To give dominion over all created things
To earthling folk: lest they should
Take themselves too seriously,
I'll give them music and a
Sense of fun, to lighten duty and
Enliven praise.'
So in wise mercy did Creator God.
And all the seventh day, he rested,
Well content.

Equilibrium

A picture of a man,
Top hat at rakish angle,
Coat tails flying,
Arms outstretched,
Riding a unicycle
Along a telegraph wire.

Risky.

Balance is achieved
Not only by prudently
Weighing alternatives,
Working out
Where to put our feet.
Sometimes we simply
Need to let go.

Magnificat for three choirs

Encircled by music,
Harmonies swirling from
Choir to answering choir,
Swelling at last to join in
High thanksgiving ...
It was like being
Drawn into the Rublev icon.

The three conductors,
Watching each other
With courteous attention,
Drew from each choir
Sounds of great beauty,
Invited us to join
Their creativity, and
Offer our hearts
With their Magnificat.

Written after hearing the three cathedral choirs gathered in different places in Winchester Cathedral sing Victoria's 'Magnificat' at the Southern Cathedrals Festival 1999.

Action plan

'What will you do now?'
People asked when I retired.
'Guard the space,' I said.

Thanksgiving

Given so much,
What have I done to
Deserve it?
Nothing,
Absolutely nothing.

No wonder my heart
Dances.

Index